I0760021

Spruce
to
cedar

Spruce to cedar

Lasänmą
(Mariah MacDonald)

BRICK BOOKS
PRINCE EDWARD COUNTY, ONTARIO

Library and Archives Canada Cataloguing in Publication

Title: Spruce to cedar / Lasänmą (Mariah MacDonald).
Names: Lasänmą, author.
Description: Text in English with some text in Dene and Southern Tutchone.
Identifiers: Canadiana (print) 20250324865 | Canadiana (ebook) 2025032492X | ISBN 9781771316705 (softcover) | ISBN 9781771316712 (EPUB) | ISBN 9781771316729 (PDF)
Subjects: LCGFT: Poetry.
Classification: LCC PS8623.A77386 S67 2026 | DDC C811/.6—dc23

We gratefully acknowledge the Canada Council for the Arts, the Government of Canada through the Canada Book Fund, and the Ontario Arts Council and the Government of Ontario for their support of our publishing program.

 Canada Council for the Arts Conseil des Arts du Canada

Funded by the Government of Canada | Canada

The book is set in Punto and Aboriginal Serif.
Design by Kilby Smith-McGregor.

Though much of the work of Brick Books takes place on the ancestral lands of the Anishinaabeg, Haudenosaunee, Huron-Wendat, and Mississaugas of the Credit peoples, our editors, authors, and readers from many backgrounds are situated from coast to coast to coast in Canada on the traditional and unceded territories of over six hundred nations who have cared for Turtle Island from time immemorial. While living and working on these lands, we are committed to hearing and returning the rightful imaginative space to the poetries, songs, and stories that have been untold, under-told, wrongly told, and suppressed through colonization.

for my Ä́ghàałan
for the inspiration
for making me into the person i am today
for raising me the best you knew how
for the good times
for the hard times
for the past
for the future

Shäw Níthän

in loving memory

Mary Shadow (Ätsk'ia) • 1929–2009
Marge Jackson (Chùschwa) • 1918–2013
Jenny Moose (Däts'ä'la) • 1920–2015
Agnes MacDonald-Sutton (Ts'ùk'aymą) • 1946–2022
Delmer MacDonald (Gáts'äda) • 1965–2024

Lasänmą says:

it feels like a "honey in red rose tea" type of day . . .

Ä̗kụ, 2004

a wood stove intentionally dented
so one can cook on top.
a few feet over sits a bunk bed fit for four.
the tv sits snug on the kitchen table.

insulation, wood dust, & paint fumes linger into the night.
by morning our lungs have no air, our body has no soul.

letters fly back & forth,
a plea for housing till the work is done;
& every time, the cold response:
you can't be assisted,
as we must abide by the housing policy.[1]

because a suitable environment for children isn't the priority here.

a commotion to finish the bathroom,
to relieve us from the outhouse;
& eventually, we'll be pissing in a doorless lavatory,
with taps that don't bring water.

Semo hauls jugs of water into the white cavalier,
we drive carefully down the alaska hwy.
she boils pots atop the beaten wood stove
& carries buckets upstairs for our bath.
construction workers leave behind half-ass jobs. knobs screwed in wrong.
hot is cold,
cold is hot,
a cracked window in the main bedroom, a deck with no railings,
& more.
it doesn't matter *as long as we abide*
by the housing policy.

the siding will be unfinished for the next fifteen years,
leaving room for rot & mould
to manifest in childhood bedrooms.

1 *"The house must be at occupancy stage within the first year of funding."*

when i was five, Ắtà showed Ắmbada & me how to snare rabbits.
he took us out on a winter morning, bright & early,
& we trekked around the yard looking for tracks.
he showed us what rabbit tracks looked like & how to gently
step over the path
so the rabbits wouldn't know we'd been there.
Ắtà showed us how to set the snare
& how to place brush around it to ensure the trap would work.

we must have set fifteen snares under the setting sun.
the next morning we headed out into the crisp cold air.
we caught five rabbits that day,
so we reset the traps & continued to check on them daily.

out of all the rabbits, we only kept one.
the rest were given to the elders in town,
Ắmbada & i received many hugs & blessings.

months later, Ắmbada & i were trick-or-treating
when we reached one of the elders' homes, Ätsk'ia.
her eyebrows jumped over her glasses when she saw us.
i have something for you two!
she came back with two pairs
of beautifully sewn mittens
lined with rabbit fur.

pb&j for me just jam for Ấmbada
we smother whitebread
squishing slices together
adding another sandwich to the pile

we harvest blankets
burgundy tea sets
& our favourite stuffies
we set up a picnic on the balcony
with no rails

the balcony that does not exist anymore
torn down in the renovation
that came too late

sitting on the rickety boards we eat
gently placing pieces into the mouths of our teddy bears
while we watch Ấtà working on a truck outside
radio blaring behind him
bepsi jingles & weather reports
he ducks under the black truck with the painted flames on the hood
even though we all know it is destined for the graveyard

we scared you straight
when i was in grade 2
Ắmbada in grade 3
a demonstration of pigs' lungs happened at school
blackened tar-filled organs struggling to
breathe   ingrained in my seven-year-old psyche—
we followed you outside to the porch
sitting side by side on the steps
we begged you to stop
we needed a parent
we didn't want you to get sick
you asked us why we asked you instead of Ắtà
we told you we knew he wouldn't listen
but you would

& you did

Semo says:

i just want you girls to be happy

raspberries taste like Łu Ghą
like two sisters hovering over bushes
fingers stained pink
plucking fresh red berries
under the summer sun
general assemblies
fishing camps
Ắtsųą's cabin
sockeye salmon stream
windy days
Chùschwa's store
selling beaded earrings
a bridge that must never be crossed because—
a bear might get you!
flip flops & learning how to tie shoes
Ắtà's burl bowl kiosk
tourist taking pictures
without asking me
so they can go home
& tell their friends
look, a real indian!
fishing gaffs hung on the wall
burl wood countertops
& dollar store coffee mugs
candlelit nights
card games   crib & go fish
silent snores
i peek out from under covers
stories of bigfoot keep me awake
if i fall asleep
surely he'll kidnap me
another sunny day rears its head
Semo says—
don't eat the raspberries! they're dirty!
two sisters sneakily hover over bushes
fingers stained pink
plucking fresh red berries
peeking over shoulders
before they feast

a bathtub filled to the brim with dirt
leans against the porch steps, waiting for the warm
comforting breeze,
for the petrichor-filled afternoons,
when the spruce trees bud,
& crocuses take bloom.

it takes a day. Semo sits back,
coffee in hand studying how Ắtà teaches.
two wild-haired children hover over shoulder
watching potatoes, carrots, green beans, & tomatoes[2]
sewn into soil.

in a blink of an eye
carrots breach soil,
vines curl around porch railings,
& the potatoes are still nestled comfortably in dirt.
Ắtà comes out to harvest,
for dinner they enjoy moose & vegetable stew.

---

2 *weed*

i crave a winter night
driving to the convention center
watching how the lights of the town
                    illuminate the dark

i miss the silence of crisp mountain air
i want the hum coming from inside
while i linger near the door

the warmth of the community feast
the feeling as i find Ắtsųą sitting next to Ắtsų Khįą

icy tarmac
snow flurries
vancouver snowstorm jostling the plane as we take off
i'm flung about on my seat
horrified faces painted on
strangers

& i'm

smiling   taken back to
spring 2008
driving in the bush
imaginary roads
willows whipping the truck bed
scraping along windows
as we're shaken about
on our hunt for burl bowls

a loud, boisterous laugh can be heard down the room,
the aroma of moose stew drifts down the hall,
hunger seeps in, despite the numerous snacks laid out on plastic-lined tables.
stacks of pilot bread wait to be covered in margarine or homemade jam,
designed to be dipped into an elder's tea, till soft & moist.
hooligan eggs are handed out,
nestled in between tree needles,
waiting for little cuzzins to sprinkle salt on top,
destined to pop
between toddler teeth.
wildflowers sit in dollar store vases,
ready to be stolen into big purses,
tucked in between prescribed medicine, strawberry candies, & loose coins.

next to the kitchen, near the coffee cart
aunties & uncles mingle, circulating gossip.
children's pitchy screams can be heard outside.
dads & grandfathers watch their young from afar
as they finish their pack of smokes for the day.

once the cooks yell
we need wolf volunteers!
hundreds of bowls are prepared.
aunties & uncles disappear from the coffee cart,
grandfathers yell at their descendants to come eat—
at the potlatch we'll feast as one,
in the memory of the one we lost.

it's sockeye eggs collected in buckets
gifted to elders later that night

it's Ắtà's chainsaw
wood dust snowflakes
cracking & snapping of spruce trees
crashing to the ground

it's halloween pillowcases
children running in groups down the village rd
cheap polyester costumes
stretched over puffer jackets & snow pants

it's an auntie cackling in the potlatch house
gossiping over pilot bread & tea
granny scarfs adorning their scalps
purple   pinks   & orange

it's Ắtà's wood truck
early morning drives
carpenter vest hanging on the driver seat
dreamcatcher hanging on rearview mirror
dreamcatcher tattooed on his forearm

it's raising the future generation under loving arms
choosing to thrive in western society
despite the systems set against us

it's the colour of resiliency
the colour of living   despite the terrors of the past

the sweet smell fills the basement,
long moose strips hang from the ceiling.
rays of light shine through the window
& the strips glow red.

it may not be how Ǻtsų Khįą would make it,
but this will do for now.
if we were to put the strips outside,
there's no doubt in Ǻtà's mind
that the dogs would devour them.

they've been hanging for days,
& every morning
i stare up at them—daydreaming
i could snap a piece off
                                        dip it in margarine
                                                                        & let the salt dance.

but they're not ready.

i walk & weave under them.
hopefully they'll be ready soon,
so i can taste the sweet Ätthän Gän.

gravel rd with no end
a white van   dubbed *war pony*
leaves dust clouds
in its wake
wheels catching every bump
& pothole
nausea
the stench of walmart plastic bags
burns nose hairs
as i wait for the moment
the gravol doesn't work
suitcases jostle
next to a red cooler
mackenzie hwy
is a gravel rd
with no end

i only visited you a few times—
when I was young,
when Semo would take us on trips
down bison-filled dirt rds.

the last time Ä́tà came along,
we stayed for a week or two
& when we left
it was six in the morning.

we packed up the war pony
under the Dehcho fog
before climbing up white porch steps
to say goodbye.

i'd only seen you with your hair up,
hidden under scarves or wrapped in claw clips.
you'd just woken up & long silver hair flowed down your back.
i was entranced.

elders at home didn't have long hair;
they dyed their greys,
permed their hair
curly & short.

under the early morning silence
& Semo's silent tears as she hugged you
i realized i could be beautiful
with shining silver hair
just like my Setsų Cho.

the clay nestles underneath my fingernails
i claw my way effortlessly up the clay cliffs
behind the yukon inn
i am nine   & other children climb next to me
i don't know what awaits at the end
but a spirit in a wooden medicine mask stops me
where do you think you're going?
it's not your time yet
my fingers are pried away
dried rubble lets loose
& i
f
a
l
l
l
l
l
l
l
l

into my bed

the sun set at four,
children coming out of school knew they only had an hour
before dark.
i never had a problem with it;
children only know the reality they grow up in.

but it was different on hockey nights.
after Åmbada's practice
we walked out into
the dark.
silence paired with the hum of the fluorescents
& the crunch of snow under boots.
i was okay under the town lights,
there was a pattern as we drove.
light to dark
                    light to dark
                                        light to dark
                                                            light to dark

then it was just me & the stars,
a staring match with the void.

To: Lasänmą, 2009

you restless soul, not a clue in the world, still wearing your rose-coloured glasses; though the tint is beginning to fade. your brain is on fire, you sit up late into the night looking out your dirty window to the moon. you let fear turn electric, running down your pitchforked veins, sending goosebumps down your arms & down your spine. the tv says you're going to die in three years, the world is going to open up & swallow you whole & there's nothing you can do to stop it. Ắtà jokes that we'll run away to K'uą Män & survive off the land & this only adds fuel to a roaring fire. *1000 ways to die* blares on the tv, stories of unlikely death sneaking into your dreams, keeping you awake at night. you're scared, you ask yourself *what is on the other side?* you've barely lived a decade, yet you are already pondering the great beyond.

you worry for a future that hasn't started, you worry for yourself, for Ắghàałan, for the world. you begin to picture planets aligning in 2012 to cause biblical implications. these worries seep into your dreams, follow you both day & night. you try to find support in these moments of dread & are promptly brushed off: *you are too young to worry like this . . . too young to carry the weight of the world . . . too young to understand . . .* you suffer through these emotions alone, often staying up late into the night, pondering the void from the back seat of late car rides, constantly imagining apocalyptic futures.

if i could travel back in time for you, i would. there is nothing to worry about; you'll be fine, & your family will be fine in the way you know it to be fine. i would tell you the world will continue spinning after the mayan calendar ends in 2012. the end-of-the-world bullshit is made for people who can't think for themselves. i'll tell you to quit worrying about things that are out of your control; despite me continuing the same habits. (though now my worrying isn't about fictional apocalypses but rather the somewhat rational fear of people around me disappearing from my life.)

Lasänmą, we are one & we carry our legacy of rabbit-hole worry to this very day; despite the knowledge that this constant worrying is irrational. i double-check that our stove isn't on before i leave & triple-check that my door is locked. i risk missing my bus to run back to my third-floor apartment to double-check one more time because i too fear the worst. i repeat lines in my head like a prayer before bed, hoping that i don't wake up to memorial posts on facebook. i check that my hair straightener isn't plugged in despite knowing it's tucked away in the bathroom drawer. i can see these worries in you as i stay up late into the night thinking about my future, thinking about climate change, thinking about how there's a possibility i'll never have children due to the ice caps melting, due to the rise in seas, due to the greed of rich white capitalists. i wonder if i could've ever worried like this if it wasn't for you worrying alone in your room thirteen years ago, looking out into the night sky scared for the last three years of your nine-year-old life; & i wish you didn't have to be alone.

From: Lasänmą, 2023

blades glide on ice
the light post illuminates our path

Semo circles around me
demonstrating beginner's figure skating
i fumble behind
our legs weaving in & out
creating loopy lines in the ice
our conversation echoing off barricades
drifting out into the village streets
snow lightly drifts around us
building a barrier over time
from ice to blade

& with snow-covered blades
we end our lesson

Ą̈tsųą, 2011

the night your house burned down
i was dreaming of my eleventh birthday.
you came through a smoking door
asking—begging—for help.
i didn't know what to do,
& once you realized it was fruitless
you left through the smoking door.
i woke up to Ą̈tà turning on the bedroom light.

Ą̈tà sped into town
& when the charred home came to view
a police car began tailing us down the village rd.
rage boiled in Ą̈tà
as he stepped out of the car, yelling
i am not drunk, my fucking mother's house just burned down!
Ą̈tà mocked a balancing test in anger,
swearing at the police as they drove away.

burnt plastic, wood, & memories
stunk up the morning air.
you were fine, Ą̈tsía was safe too.
but the air still felt different,
dread hung over our heads
as we visited your shaken bodies,
wondering where you were to begin.

across town
drums pound intensely
vibrating energy from the hall
i feel it in my soul
elders sit on fold-up chairs
watching stick gambling unfold
men sit in two parallel lines
as they move to the beat
creating positive energy
aiming for the win
outside children run down
gravel rds
horseflies wreak havoc
biting chunks
of tanned flesh
i escape into the northern store
on the hunt for bepsi & ice cream bars

Dehcho flows gently
spirits sing to me softly
in water ripples

saskatoon trees & rez dogs
"diamonds" by rihanna
end-of-the-world christmas
spent praying in a circle
around the campfire
in Setsų's backyard

Ắtà says:

you can trust a wolf
you know what they are thinking
you can trust a bear
you know what they are thinking
you can't trust a human
you'll never know what they are thinking

who has the right indigenous land?[3]

Ắtà is prepping the skidoo as a car pulls up to the cabin.
a scientist steps out of the passenger side.

hello, my name is . . .

Ắtà isn't welcoming to this man.
his toothless grin vanishing, eyes narrowing towards this stranger.
he flicks ash from his cigarette;
Ắtà has his guard up,
like at the store when the cashier was following us
or the few times he stomped his steel-toed boots in my school.

we just wanted bring to you attention,
that your traps are interfering with our research . . .

the rumble of the skidoo fills the rifts of silence.
i look up to Ắtà wondering if he'll explode.

we're just down the road a bit . . .
we have written permission from the owner to research on this land—

permission from my mother!
this is our land you're on.
Ắtà argues
his cigarette hanging from his lips.

well . . . your traps are interfering with our studies—
i have a written note here if you want to—

your studies are interfering with our traps.

the scientist's lips form a flatline.
his annoyance translates to heavy breathing
pictured in the frost coming from his nose.

---

3 *K'uą Män*

you know, i have a right to be here—

he points up to Nàday Gän

my great, great, grandfather named that mountain—

Nàday Gän had a name long before your fucking grandpa 'discovered it'

when you're a child
you don't understand why you're not allowed to sit in the front seat.
when you're a child
you don't understand why you can't get the same tattoo as Ắtà.
when you're a child
you don't understand why you can't eat all the Ätthän Gän in one sitting.
when you're a child
you don't understand why you're not allowed to eat oatmeal
with the dinosaur eggs.
when you're a child
you don't understand why Ắtà can't step foot inside the school
to attend award ceremonies or christmas concerts.
when you're a child
you don't understand why Ắtà yelled at his 'teacher' in the airport,
or why rage & pain lingered in his eyes for the rest of the night,
his hands gripping the steering wheel.
the usually cranked radio turned low.

how do you tell a child
that if they were born in a different time
they would have been taken?
how do you tell a child
that if they were born in a different time
they would have been abused?
how do you tell a child
that if they were born in a different time
they would
be ashamed?
how do you tell a child
that *you* were born in a different time?

the warmth drenches my hands & i go all in
i pull at an organ & a cuzzin helps me out
snowsuits covered in slick blood
skidoo idling nearby
we're next to an old cabin at K'uą Män
the snow around us holds organs   hide   & fur
it's twenty-five below   yet i still sweat
i refrain from wiping my brow
in fear of blood sticking to my forehead
Ǻghàałan watch in the distance
talking over cigarettes
calling reinforcements
bargaining which parts to give as payment
for the cuzzin or uncles to help
others dig in canvas bags
finding the right tools
preparing for the next steps
of this moose harvest

To: Lasänmą, 2013

i'm not going to say the pain goes away, but it gets easier to live with. i am not going to lie to you & say that this moment in time isn't difficult, because it is. it's a big change for you. moving to Kwänlin is jarring at first, you're so used to the secluded woods, the trees surrounding the house, like a barrier protecting you from the outside world. you are not alone anymore, & i know it is scary. but you'll get used to this. you'll get used to the streetlights peeking through the curtains, you'll get used to the sounds of cars passing by in the middle of the night, & the moments when you bump into your neighbours outside. you'll always be searching for Ą́kų, & i am sorry to say, it'll never be the same again. you'll go home one day & realize that the house isn't made for you anymore, the familiar carpets & blue walls are no longer yours to claim.

you're going to be stubborn, it is a trait we both have. you're going to move back to Dákwäkäda for grade nine. you're going to meet depression. i'm not going to lie to you. you'll listen to slander against your parents, about how you weren't raised right. you'll become a therapist for a heartbroken Ą́tà. you'll feel like you're stepping on eggshells for the first time in your life. you'll be forced to grow up in a few short months. *pure heroine*, lorde's first album, will lull you to sleep in your cold room in the basement. her dark tones will make you feel understood. a teacher will sit you down on a bench in the hallway one day & ask if you're doing ok. you'll fight with the tears as they pour out of you, & you'll wonder how life changed so quickly within a year.

you are going to try something stupid. you are going to find a spot behind the village in the woods, & you are going to lay there in the freezing winter snow. you want to die. but you're going to have more life after that. life will slowly get better, the pain will numb & you'll survive. your stubbornness will take you far in life, you'll be told you can't achieve the life you dream of. you'll prove them all wrong, & win awards along the way. you'll find people who will understand you, you'll find people who don't. you'll find people who will use you, & you'll find the strength to leave them. you are strong, even when you don't mean to be.

i am not going to lie to you. you're going through one of the worst years of your life. but you'll make it through; & because you were able to make it through such hardships at such a young age, i know that i can make it through rough times. when those dark moments creep into my mind, those days when i just want to stay in bed & rot away, i know i have resilience within me because you survived, so i'll survive now, ten years down the line . . . we survive.

From: Lasänmą, 2023

you sink drunkenly onto the kitchen floor
tears trickling down your stubble
bangs curling over your forehead covering your shame
as you cradle a budweiser for comfort

i watch
not knowing what to do
not knowing why i have to be your therapist
i'm only 14

Dákwäkäda, 2014

i did my research,
it would be comfortable—
peaceful.

i watch the skyline,
i am waiting to die. spruce
trees shade my resting
place, every now & then a gust
of wind knocks clusters of
snow off branches—
frttt thump. frttt thump.

frozen breath caresses flushed cheeks.
impatient, i wait under frosted eyelashes
& snot dripping down
philtrum. i really want to
give up.

the roar of a skidoo echoes in the trees around me,
a sound that i can hear when i think about home.
the grumble of the machine stops at my feet,
familiar skidoo gas permeating in the air.

it's your skidoo

i paused
i thought he was just letting me borrow it

really?

of course!

A̋tsía always had my back
i'm sure he could see
the tears i hid at night
for the few short months
i stayed under their care
A̋tsųą & A̋tsía ensured
i was happy
every night i was outside
finding new purpose
in layers of sweatpants
& hand-me-down helmets
flying down bush trials
driving donuts in parking lots
screaming
    gripping on for dear life
when i'd
accidentally hit a jump
    & fly

the blood in my veins falls quiet
lulled by waves
voices in my head soften
algae-covered roçks
waves lapping over toes
ravens singing unique sets
dragonflies race by
thwip of fishing line
plop of fish hook
& a game of patience
mosquitos whizzing
bees buzzing
purple aurora flourishing
the curious camp robber flitting up & down
the fight
thrashing water
tense muscles
dragging whitefish out of lake foam
whack
dead eyes
(watchful eyes—
of a seagull)
fingers slip under gills
added to the pile
tobacco in the waves
when i'm done
Shäw Níthän creator
for the blessing
Shäw Níthän whitefish
for providing
fish gutted
entrails thrown in water
seagulls screaming
thrashing
claws reaching
calling out to me
for more
more
more

Däts'ä'ala

weary joints   weakening fingers   blurry eyes

the dread as your life's work is taken away
growing older is an honour
however   there is misery in not being able to weave bead
                                        to thread
                                to push needle through
                                        hide
sewing was your livelihood
from the construction of the alaska hwy
to the birth of your Ä̋shèa Ke
you were a businesswoman
stationed at K'ų̀a Män
taking orders from construction workers
in 1942

expertly tacking down beads
                into intricate designs
the tension of your thread was impeccable
                your fingers calloused from decades of work
knowledge overflowing
                passed down to generations of beaders
your artwork pristine
your fingers shaking
your precision thinning
your vision wavering
your life passion slowly stolen by age

moments of you

sparkle in my eyes when i find the perfect jean jacket
denim stitched with february skies
embedded with chainsaw gas & wood dust
pride in my heart   red ac/dc logo branded on chest
cotton   grey like the alaska hwy
work trucks with bloated speakers fly past
leaving electric guitar solos echoing in the treeline
nostalgic ears pricked   an old rusted truck gurgles down the street
exhaust clouds like frosty december mornings
radio blabbing weather reports
. . . whitehorse   teslin   atlin   haines junction & the kluane lake region . . .
cigarette cravings, second-hand
desperately breathing in polluted air
—claiming i don't have a problem afterwards
bangs   curling over my forehead
just like yours used to
not that long ago

Ắkų̀,2016

fresh renovations
siding finally completed
15 yrs down the line
rickety deck disappeared
door turned into wall
light fixture left behind
left with no purpose
other than as evidence
of what was

bathroom sinks
bring forth water
grey-blue painted porch
cigarette-stained
walls & carpet

Lasänmą says:

every time i come home it feels like a relapse

is home found in cable tv droning on all day
& all night

is home found in an unfinished basement
covered floor to ceiling with memories
pictures stapled to walls
beer bottles lined up onto shelves
proudly displayed to the drywall

is home found in the forest
in the middle of nowhere
discovered down dirt rds
turn left at the next telephone pole
guarded by friendly rez dogs

is home found in Ằtà's spaghetti sauce
or in Semo's birthday cakes
with the smarties on top

is home found in paint-chipped stairs
worn & weathered
steep & rickety
heart attack with every step

is home found in found in dog yards
unfinished treehouses
& half-built barbeque pits

small-town life is beautiful
the gas station's just a bike ride away
the village bakery sells the world's sweetest danishes
& frosty's has the bluest iceberg desert
you can get lost in the mountains
as they loom over you
thousands travel here just to witness this beauty

i was lucky enough to be raised here
to witness halloween fireworks
the christmas tree decorations dancing from light posts
to watch the leaves bloom every spring
& fall in autumn
yet your brain could rot in the toxicity
of the Kwǟntsi̇̀ Mèn

legs stretched out spinning the latest gossip
entangling people in the strands of venom
striking pinchers, sucking confidence
weaving stories of lies
truths
& half-truths

don't get caught in the Kwǟntsi̇̀ Mèn
you'll be the hottest topic of the week
isolated ensnared monitored
eight beady eyes watching your every move
trapped in silk & suffocated
truths
& half-truths

my Ǟghàałan
entangled once before
rumours & gossip echoed down
band office walls
pincers ready to snap & legs ready to wrap
entangled in the lies
truths
& half-truths

Jenída
almost feels like home
am i destined to die alone?
long bus rides
[4]

4 am instagram stories
watching from the comfort
of the comforter
why am i never worthy?
unread messages
exploitation of your body
to feel loved
though the feeling is fleeting
visiting home
this space is no longer yours
cigarette stains
& ashtrays homemade
out of abalone shells

---

4 *silence*

Ä̋tsų̨ą̨, 2018

i walk down the hall roses in hand
i heard of your condition
i didn't want to but i came anyway
not that i am a terrible person
i just wanted to avoid
the heartache
&
the moment
when your eyes didn't recognize mine

i spot your permed greys
you're sitting in a wheelchair

who are you?

your eyes see right through me

mariah

who?

blinking back tears
i try again
maybe you might remember in Dän K'e
you've always preferred that name

Lasänmą̨

who?

To: Lasänmą, 2017

the sun is a terrifying beast that brings life & death. i suppose it's all in how you choose to see her. she could be good, she could be evil, she could be both for all i care. summers are turning hotter, & winters are turning to slush as snow melts in december & spring slowly creeps into the year sooner than expected; every fucking year. you've turned into a full-blown climate activist, spreading the message on facebook. screaming into an abyss where no one cares. your anxiety simmers in your gut as you watch the news pour in over the years & you start to turn paranoid.

the talk of the summer is the eclipse. warnings are posted everywhere, everyone needs proper eye protection. Kwänlin isn't the best location in the world to watch this event, but you make do with what you have. you've accidentally glanced at the sun & now you're paranoid, wondering if you've fucked your vision for life. you wait a week before you decide you're fine, but the persistent voice in the back of your head won't let the anxious feeling in your gut go. you lay awake late into the night wondering if you're going to be ok, you begin to think about death. you begin to spiral. this isn't the first time you've pondered the great unknown, & it certainly isn't your last. but this fear is fresh, it hits different areas of your brain, & you wonder if your spirit feels pain after death. if the afterlife is only pain, would you even remember that you were alive once? these thoughts burrow a hole in your chest, & you wonder who would even care if you were gone. only Semo would feel the full impact, she's the only one who cares.

you know more now than you did at nine. you now know how to release these feelings in your heart. you create a short story about death, releasing your thoughts into keyboards & blue light screens. you lock this story in your laptop, letting it simmer in a hidden folder, buried deep within your desktop. you do all this while staying up late into the night & sleeping away the day. you turn into a recluse—more so than you already were. you ask Semo for a therapist as you hide under blankets, covering your shame. before you know it you're talking to a stranger—complimentary juice box in hand—& they're diving into the wrong subjects, picking at all the wrong parts of your brain; leaving you to work on this issue alone. you'll figure this out alone, just like you've always done.

you don't see much of a future ahead of you. you never thought you would make it this far. you've already finished high school, won awards, & achieved all the accomplishments you thought you'd never gain. you consider yourself an adult despite still being a child. you already think your life is over, where do you go from here? the sun will continue to grow hotter, & people will continue not to care despite the situation's urgency. you'll continue to wonder if there is a future ahead of you, though you'll eventually accept death as it is. the end goal. the final marker. everything must come to an end, even you, & when it does come you will be terrified. you'll start a new journey into the unknown, & hopefully it'll be a peaceful one. you haven't worried about death since, & hopefully you'll never turn existential again. though i'm not going to make any promises to you, just yet . . .

From: Lasänmą, 2023

Ámbada talks about partying there—
in the cabin that holds our childhoods
like that connection means nothing
like our hopes & dreams didn't live embedded in the wood logs
nestled in the burl countertops
buried in the floorboards
hidden in dollar store cups
plucked off raspberry bushes
& squashed

blue walls   blue carpet
puppy stickers & thumbtack holes
sharpie graffiti on my dresser
nivea pearly shine lip balm
late-night infomercials
tv static   peace lilies   golden pothos
great-grandma’s curtains & china cabinet
yellow lab   klondike   sits on the porch peering in windows
Ä́tsųą’s dining table   dinner set for 4
Ä́tà’s stir-fry   ramen noodles mixed into fried vegetables & soya—

cigarette-stained walls   cigarette-scented carpet
sun-faded puppy stickers & thumbtack holes
my dresser long gone   destined for the landfill
nivea pearly shine lip balm in my purse   reminder of home
late-night infomercials
hd flat screen   peace lilies   neon pothos
great-grandma’s curtains in Semo’s care
great-grandma’s cabinet in mine
yellow lab   klondike   ashes rest in yard
Ä́tsųą’s dining table   dinner set for 1
Ä́tà’s stir-fry   ramen noodles mixed into fried vegetables & soya—

anxieties hurl from my chest
engine is still warm &
it's just you & me
under the cover
of a november night

we should've gone inside
ten minutes ago
yet you sit
& listen
hunting for ways to solve my problems
despite me only wanting your ear to listen
i can't recall what we've talked about
but Semo therapy sessions always
feed my soul

Semo

long hair tucked & curled
into claw clips
baby hairs curling
over your forehead
glasses slipping down your Dene nose
as you focus on creating
something new

beads to leather
yarn to hook
charms to lace
all these projects
yet your shimmer polish
remains unscathed

the river swirls gently down
if i didn't know better   i'd consider it safe to swim
i rest on a bench   blisters forming on my soles

across the river   construction workers cuss
drills & hammers echo down toward me
three birds swoop down   diving at the water
yet flying upwards at the last second
avoiding being swept away

the river flows past me   i keep an eye out for fish
but all i see is stones
the sun beats down & i wonder if i'll get a tan if i sit here all day
the shrill phone alarm reminds me i have somewhere to be
the second of serenity broken
as i push myself back onto my blistered feet

medicine
flows in her veins
she sees me
watching me as if she's known me
since birth
silver hair flows down her spine
from the lands Semo was born in
a Dene elder
purple paints my aura
she tells me to keep working
on myself
on my culture
on my spirituality
she tells me i'm on the right path
& i find comfort
in her brown eyes

i tell myself i'll be happier in the city

i tell myself i'll be happier underneath blossom trees

i tell myself i'll be happier alone in my apartment

i tell myself i'll be happier away from family

i tell myself i'll be happier tomorrow

i tell myself i'll be happier in the spring

i tell myself i'll be happier next year

i tell myself i'll be happier back home

i tell myself i'll be happier bearing forty below

i tell myself i'll be happier alone in the woods

i tell myself i'll be happier closer to family

i tell myself i was happier yesterday

i tell myself i'll be happier in the fall

i tell myself—

Ắtà says:

don't live in the city   if ṣhit hits the fan they're all like ants
scrambling to get out of their ant hills
the freeways will be packed
with nowhere to go

from
spruce to cedar
snow to rain
mountains to skyscrapers
i'm heading home

Ấndaya says:

what do you mean you're home?

vancouver's not home . . .

2021

i've never been this soaked in my life
i'll never get dry   my soul is water-logged
i'll never shake all the drops from my hair
moss will sprout out my ears
my skin embedded into cedar trees
tangled   infected with ivy
fungi will sprout out of my nail beds
& Keyi will take control
as the rain engulfs me
molds me
& spits me out new

2019

i long for early sunrise
melting through glass skyscrapers
long to be in an apartment
of my own
with a terrace view of the Keyi—
i can cover my living room
floor-to-ceiling with plants (&
more plants—like Ắtà)
& wake up with the sun
as i commute to the
university   but before i leave
i watch the sunrise
with a latte in hand
bella at my feet
waiting for scrambled eggs
& maybe bacon too
to fall underneath the
table—

2022

i long for the late sunsets
watching the sun slip behind Nàday Gän
long to be in a cabin i built
with my own money   & hands
with a wraparound porch overlooking Tsí Män
i can cover my home
floor-to-ceiling with plants (&
more plants—like Ą̈tà)
& watch the full moon in the marbled sky
as i normalize
a night in   away from town
a night of peace
but   before i sleep
i can watch the sky melt into black
a cup of red rose in hand
bella at my feet
waiting for me to come inside
into the warmth of home

Äzįzha

clouds swirled around her like oat milk in iced coffee
her aura could take me away
      cleanse me from my past
                  claim my sorrows
                        smudge my sins
                              & prepare me for
something unfamiliar
      she whispers promises of growth
                        of healing
                              of prosperity
she spies through autumn leaves
watching over us as the smoky clouds swirl in the night,
                                    marbling
underneath her light

i head down the street
i need—or want?—to clear
my head as bloated
petals fall around me
like pink snowflakes
you left this world today
the end of a chapter
i clear my throat not my head
& watch the pink petals—

Ts'ùk'aymą

spruce sap, needles, & bark.
dry meat, fish, & butter,
    moose meat rolled into sushi rolls.
the last-minute trips to burwash & haines.
the way your soft hands gripped the steering wheel
lightly jerking the car left & right—

yet you got scared when Ą̈mbada drove.

calluses cover your fingertips,
a testament to the decades of meticulous beadwork—
the slippers & vests made from your hands
as you sit at your desk with the tv on.
your strong fingers gripped mine
when i last saw you—
& i wish i'd lingered longer.

before your home turned into dust & embers
i'd play with knock-off legos
as vhs disney movies played over & over.
taco & candy, two chihuahuas
sitting strategically underneath tables
scouting for scraps, while
Ą̈mbada & i waited patiently for you to leave the kitchen
so we could open & close the fridge door
to see the light turn on & off
because Ą̈tà removed the bulb in ours.

you'd take us on laundry trips,
paying us with vending machine pops
& trips to frosty's
where we'd sit in your indigo van
& people-watch as we ate vanilla soft serve.

on easter & christmas, we gathered
at Ä́tsų Khį̨ą's home by the lake,
& during potlatches, you'd make sure i ate
hooligan, fish, eggs, & pilot bread.
during halloween
we'd visit your house & you'd give us extra chips
as you & Ätsía *ooed* & *awed* over our costumes.

you took me in at fourteen,
giving me a reprieve from life.
giving me lessons in Dän K'e
& room to breathe without error,
                                                  without consequence.

you showed me medicine—
spruce sap, needles, & bark.
you fed me
dry meat, fish & butter,
    moose meat rolled into sushi rolls.

how to say i love you in Dän K'e:

1. taking down a moose in the fall
    a. harvesting its meat
    b. a gift to the community
2. keeping some moose for your Ǻghàałan
    a. cutting meat into strips
    b. hanging it over the woodstove   in the basement
    c. until dry
3. showing your Ǻdzų̈a secrets
    a. where you pick blueberries
    b. where you harvest whitefish
4. sewing your little ones moccasins   mitts   & vests
    a. wolves beaded into hide & fur
5. fixing an extra plate at the potlatch
    a. because you couldn't make it to the feast
6. climbing up the hill next to the mountains
    a. roses in hand   gift   for my Ǻghàałan
7. wrestling during ufc fight nights
    a. commercial break showdowns where the adults tickle
    b. & children punch
8. Ǻtà taking me on nature walks
    a. teaching me spruce & willow medicine
    b. teaching me how to trap rabbits
9. packing Ätthän Gän into lunch boxes
    a. with spam sandwiches & bepsi
10. wearing Ǻtsų Khįą's headscarf
    a. paired with my biggest pair of beaded earrings

Lasänmą's google search history:

can i become dependent on tylenol?

hunching over a bag of grease & salt
shoveling fries & sauce into my mouth
no thoughts
no feelings
just hunger
just pain
in my abdomen
in my leg
in my left foot
a day of non-stop non-fat lattes
no time to think
i'm a manufacturing machine
steaming milk
queuing shots
pouring
placing a lid over lazy latte art
i'm granted 30 minutes to myself
& the time ticks down
as i rest
my head
my heart
my soul

i avoid prescription pills
the ones that run electricity in your veins
the ones that fill your head with helium
the ones that erase the pain entirely
i toss the doctor's note & suffer instead
i don't want to become dependant
i don't want to fulfill the prophecy
i don't want to lose myself to my own mind

my persistence
guts sliced into
rotten organ removed
fresh stitches embedded in skin
a help call button hanging next to iv drips
i crawl
scrape
struggle
out
freeing myself from the bed with the buttons
only god knows what they do

my pride
squatting in the corner
knowing i should call for help
knowing i'd rather die than be helped
wondering what will happen if it overflows
worrying about what i'll do
leaving half-full bedpan

my pain

waddling back to bed
gown draping over my shoulder
iv cart following me like i'm a dog on a leash
& it is my owner
i crawl
scrape
struggle
in
settling in the bed with the buttons
only god knows what they do

my plight
shifting in sheets
pride still intact
but a bit bruised
like the last apple lost in the bottom of my fridge
brown & unwanted

Uyètaákwätth'ät

millions of lists
filled with things to do
crumpled in the depths my my bag

Uyètaákwätth'ät

piles of laundry
piles of dishes
piles of blankets
over top of me
glued to my phone

Uyètaákwätth'ät

stacks of textbooks
filled agenda
hunched over the desk
compiling another list to be ignored

Uyètaákwätth'ät

unfulfilled academic potential
zoning in & out of conversations
praying to be released
from the confines
of my mind

Uyètaákwätth'ät

days turn into weeks
seconds into hours
how does time slip so easily from my grasp?

Uyètaákwätth'ät

matcha in a stolen band office mug
trying to not to succumb
to all-nighter insanity
eyes red & drying
over blue light screens

brown sugar & oat milk
help me cope
heart pouring over another essay
about intergenerational trauma
because my life depends on it

i haven't heard the ring of a drum
in a long time
i stand in the corner
drink in one hand
sweat in the other
i watch the dancers take the stage
singing in the tongue & voice of our ancestors
& under my breath
i sing along—
the sound from my childhood
handkerchiefs
button blankets
fur & hide
painted drums fill the room
to the beat of my heart
to the sound of my soul
resonating with the blood in my veins
methodical rhythms bring clarity
lips quivering   fingers shaking
looking down at my drink
avoiding eye contact
yearning for comfort
yearning for community
yearning to come home
yearning to know where i belong
wishing i didn't have to go[5]

5 *everywhere you go there you are . . .*

K'ày
sprinkling medicine in the tub
sore muscles soaking
knowledge from my ancestors

K'ày
harvesting branches
in the spring rain
others whisper of trauma

K'ày
i can't bear the sight
of those whipping branches
digging into my back

K'ày
western society turning medicine
into weapons
foraged from ignorance

K'ày
making jars of epsom salt with willow bark
hoping to mend decade-old wounds
medicine from my ancestors

Lasänmą says:

life is only worth living in the fall . . . [6]

6 *. . . i change my mind*
life is only worth living when it's not summer . . .

indigenous girl autumn

Dät'äl
warm blood-drenched hands
tobacco to the gums
Shäw Níthän for this blessing
skinning hide from body
harvesting muscles & organs
using every piece as the creator intended

Däts'al
smoke of the fire embedded into hair
into the fabric of my jean jacket
into my soul
Łu Gän hanging in long strips
over smoke & flames

Jänǹthù
spruce bark
the swing of an axe
cracking & snapping of wood
two wild-haired children
collect from the pile of firewood
huffing & puffing
dragging heavy logs into the basement

Dätthäw
school bus parked
on the shoulder of the alaska hwy
waiting for two girls to enter
poplar leaves atop Tsí Män
colour the once-green landscape
in the month of harvest

Jänńtl'ą̈rą
lake water
rippling under steel
violently rocking back & forth
two men struggle to tug on the net
we who sit grab at the ends
leading nets filled with fish into storage bins

Khàdlų̈ Dädäla
month of harvest
stains fingertips
washed-out ice cream bucket
wedged between my knees
one hand plucking berries
the other shovelling them into mouth

Dädäla
snap crackle & pop
flames licking firewood
feeding on ash
bringing warmth to late-night talkers
too scared to sleep in wall tents
too scared of the lingering threat
of spiders slowly descending from beams
over sleeping faces

Jänäch'ür
hair tucked away into braids
shoved into hasty buns
tucked away so i can focus
thread tangles in my fingers
beads roll off the table
& i am going to rage soon
if i don't take a break
i've been sitting here for hours

Däk'äl
fresh snow covers fallen leaves
in the second week of october
the month when ice freezes small lakes
grandmothers brew red rose tea
a scoop or two of honey stirred in
pilot bread spread out on the table
preparing for a day indoors
as another winter begins

i haven't seen my ancestors in two years
my home a memory of vibrant greens purples & pinks
the northern lights still dance without me

recognition, 2023

sadness brews in your eyes as you
talk & for the first time i see me in
you.
i recognize the loneliness in isolation, the yearning
for belonging. i can see the regrets of the past &
the empty future. i know what it's like to feel alone,
talking to talk—hoping to hope, praying to pray
for someone to listen, someone to care.

i recognize
the yearning for a culture that doesn't feel like your own,
a part of yourself torn away from you generations before we were born.

turning away from a community of support,
so sure that you're unworthy of love & forgiveness.

the yearning for love from Ą̈ghàałan
because you were starved from the beginning.

the urge to create life through your fingers,
woodchips & dust, ink to an envelope, poems scribbled in piles on your table.

the misery wondering if there'll ever be anyone who understands,
wondering if you're destined to walk this world alone.

i recognize you. i see you because i see me within your eyes.[7]

---

7 *the apple & the tree*

To Lasänmą, 2023

you watch the sunrise through closed curtains as birds sing to each other outside your window. you're at a stage where you wonder why you can't sleep anymore & why you're always running late; ndn time running through your dna. your apartment has been taken over by piles of clothes, dishes, & junk. in moments like these you always think of what Semo once said:

your mess is like a hurricane, it happens slowly & lingers for weeks.
your sister's like a tornado, it comes quickly & unexpectedly.

during this season, the summer blues hit. seasonal depression typically would hit others in a few months from now; if you were normal you would wake up happy & ready to take on the day ahead. instead the promise of sunny days fills you with deep-seated dread, & you find yourself crying & sweating at night as you pray for autumn & winter to whisk you away. instead you force yourself to go outside into the sun for vitamin d, to take iron supplements for energy that never comes, & to force yourself to stay clear from the couch in the fear it'll swallow you whole. your manager at work will pull you aside one day to ask why you've been late constantly these past few weeks. embarrassingly you will instantly burst into tears. you will hang your head in shame, hiding red swollen eyes & respond:

i don't know why,
but it's hard to wake up.
i'm sad, & i don't know why.

your manager will tell you that you're not alone & that you can come to her, she'll understand, but deep in your chest you know she won't. she'll never understand the loneliness that comes with being an ndn in isolation. everyone has someone, a community, & you've found that you're all alone down here. you have no one, & just like the many times before, you'll be the one to pull *yourself* up, because if you don't, you'll drown.

at this time there's nothing you want more than to be surrounded by the familiar blue walls of Ấkų. despite knowing that those walls are no longer ours to cląim. you dream of walking in the field of fireweed. you wish to visit the white fireweed next to the dog houses & graveyard of trucks & minivans. if you could, you would sit under the silence of the land. listen to the whisper of bees & camp robbers. instead, you're trapped down south this dreadful july. on your walk home after work, you take a different route. in the distance magenta peeks through greenery. fireweed takes over planter boxes, bees float from one petal to the next, & one plant reaches out onto the sidewalk like it's reaching out to console you, & for a moment you think that everything will be okay. but little do you know it is just the beginning of the end. in a year you'll be visiting white hospital rooms. leading a well-used wheelchair to the smoke pit outside. buying gatorade from the vending machine. eating complementary bannock from indigenous services. sitting next to a hospital bed, holding onto weakening hands. dreading the future ahead. trying to prepare yourself for the moment when nothing will be the same. little do you know, a year from now, you'll finally have a real reason to hate july.

From: Lasänmą, 2025

i tell him to sober up—

a long pause—

he tells me if i was anybody else he would have cursed me out.
but he says he loves me, so he won't.
he says i'm right,
that he needs to smarten up.

he never got sober.

Gáts'äda

wood dust floats
in the air
layering gravel dirt
like a blanket of snow
drill bit whirring
light pressure
burl bowl concaving
spruce burl transformation
bandana respirator
dust covering hair
black band t-shirt
& steel-toed boots
dollar store sign
sanded down
etched anew
in my next life i want more ~~money~~
burl trees
red hot wood burner
scorched handwriting
yukon -:spruce burl:-
'05 by:Del
resin-covered wood
hung on basement rafters
drip drip dripping
from bent & flattened metal
bumpy backwoods trails
willows whipping truck beds
stick-shift driving
burl bowl hunting
target acquired
benign bumps
swelled & cracked bark
chainsaw *re-re-revving*
wood dust floats
in the air
layering mossy ground
like a blanket of snow

distance built from my fingers
weaving webs of isolation
sinking further into myself
until i'm swallowed whole
into couch cushions
bed duvets
& king-sized pillows—
dead phone
unanswered messages
unread emails
mascara-stained freckled cheek
nestled into jade sheets
at two in the afternoon[8]

8 *everywhere you go there you are . . .*

Great-Grandpa says:

everywhere you go   there you are . . .

Åmbada, 2024

i'll never know how she expresses herself so fluently
an explosion of emotion
can be found in her body language
how she shovels food into her mouth
when a dish is so divine
how she laughs with her whole chest
her joy contagious
how she can fill a room with tension
the slam of a door deafening
her cries piercing
her smile blinding

she watches me expectantly
in the middle of june
sitting across from me
the food she cooked sits in front of me
she expects me to explode with gratitude
i should be eating at the speed of light
moaning about how delicious
this rice & chicken curry is

my taste buds are appreciative
though i'm more reserved
i'll never be fluent in the language of emotions
i hold my tears hostage   looking to the sky   praying they go away
my laugh is timid   shy   afraid to take room
my anger is held back by the skin of my teeth
my tension trapped in between shoulder blades

how is it?
her eyes stare into mine
it's excellent   one of the best meals i've eaten this month
i like when she cooks   i like that she's found her passion
but i don't know how to express myself
in the easygoing way
that she does

it's good

the truth is i don’t know how long i’m going to last under colonized institutions. surrounded by people who’ll never understand my mindset, or who frown when i swear in Dän K’e. like speaking a dying language isn’t as cool as speaking from a settler tongue. the truth is i’m tired of sweat sticking to skin & the season changing without the temperature dropping like i’m stuck in a forever summer, like i’m in limbo. the truth is i haven’t seen my ancestors in almost three years now, & i’ve never felt more lost. the truth is i’m still the little girl i was twenty years ago, & i want to go home. the truth is i don’t have a home anymore, the blue walls of childhood no longer mine to claim. the truth is everything has gone to shit, & i wish to be an impressionable child. i wish Ǻtà was still alive & well. i wish to see Ǻtsųą & Ǻtsía once more. i wish it was 2004 & nothing bad has happened.

an uncle jokes that this land is flat
like bannock! he says

on the plane ride
i watch as the scenery changes
as towering Yukon mountains slowly flatten
into lands sprinkled with lakes rivers   & ponds
i watch intently
as the moon peeks through morning skies
this land whispers to me in my dreams
asking me to come home

ever since the 14th
i don't know where home is anymore—
do i truly belong anywhere?
i don't feel welcome under concrete skyscrapers
in a city that never changes seasons
i don't feel welcome under the mountains that raised me
on the gravel rds i traversed in my youth
will i feel welcome on these flatlands?
with distant family that only knew me as a child?

the Dehcho whispers my ndn name
Godééah . . .
& i've ignored the calls
because everywhere i go   there i am
& i don't think i'll ever truly feel welcome
no matter where i go

on these lands
my name is Godéćah
the little sister
the familiar stranger

i have a vanishing memory
of the dirt roads of
Zhahti Kų́ę́
i'm a ghost of the past
running along the banks of
the Dehcho
while Semo reconnects
with her culture
at Setsų Cho's fish camp

i only stay here
for a few weeks
at a time
& the streets forget me
but the water remembers

the little sister
the familiar stranger
my nose Dene
my lips Dän K'e
but on these lands
my name is Godéćah

christmas dinner
prayer near the campfire
four generations of women
reunited
spruce brush nestled atop snow
we huddle close
the sun setting behind the Dehcho
i hold a bundle of tobacco in hand
all my love etched into skin
they're praying to god
& i'm praying to Ǻtà
i've been lost since he left
but i see him everywhere
i ask for guidance
i tell him i miss him
& i wish he was here
i sprinkle tobacco into the fire
& i linger behind
while distant family go inside
to eat
i stare into the flames
& allow tears to fall
onto snow & spruce needles

i visit the spaces of my childhood like a tourist
i take pictures of the cabin at Łu Ghą as though i've never stepped foot inside
as though i didn't grow up there
as though i never learned how to tie my shoes in the kitchen
as though i never ate the raspberries from the bush across the street
i drive the haines rd
to my next destination
& i capture the lakes & mountains
as though i'll never see them again
i take a turn at the junction
onto the alaska hwy
onwards to K'uą Män
i hover outside Ä̃tsų Khįą's home
summer harvests & easter dinners long since past
abandoned homes sit on this land now
memories clinging to the floorboards
i make my way down to the lake
& i wonder where the rickety dock went
tall grass sprouts from the water
creating green waves under the summer's breeze
i drive the alaska hwy
taking a turn at the junction
i lurk through Ä̃kų̀ like a museum
i don't touch the art inside
just observe the changes since my last visit
& wonder why my room doesn't feel like mine anymore
just an empty husk of what was
& what could've been

reasons to keep living:

1.
one day it'll be spring
&
the crocuses will bloom once more

she yells *i love you* across the bar—
she did this every time her shift ended before mine,
or when she visited to study & chat on her days off,
her arms extended over her head, creating a heart.

at first, i froze—
i still do sometimes,
my response stuck in my throat,
the words jagged & sharp.
i force stuttered replies,
not sure how to respond, but knowing i should.
i can't help but remember Ấtà's words:

> *i love you is too strong.*
> *i only say it when i mean it—from the heart.*
> *only to family, only to you kids*
> *& your mom.*
> *someone says they love me, i just respond*
> *all my love.*

it takes months of work & many *i love you's*
so now when she shouts across the bar,
her arms stretched over her head,
i yell back
i love you too—
because i do, & she doesn't have to be family, a wife, a girlfriend,
she can just be my friend
& as the words spill out of me, it feels right.

not everyone needs to be Äghàałan to be loved.

& i need to remember—
not everything Ấtà says is gospel.

from
cedar to spruce
rain to snow
skyscrapers to mountains
i'm heading home

the first to rebuild after fire
the first to take root
the first to stand tall
& shout
you can't bury me
the resiliency that brews in the pink & purple hues
the envy i feel of the unity
as fireweed covers the charred forest floor

i want to have the courage of a fireweed
to be as stubborn as fireweed

you are the air that blesses my lungs
the blood flowing through my veins
the water that brings life
you are the meaning
you are the reason i stay
the reason i push though
the crocuses that bloom in spring
the wind in the mountains
the rain in the clouds
the thunder in the skies
the sap dripping from spruce bark
the leaves falling in autumn painting Tsí Män yellow
you are the delicate snowflakes
drifting down Nàday Gän
you are life's greatest privilege
you are life's greatest meaning
you are my little wolf
my Ắghats'èa
my Ắghra
my future

Lasänmą says:

Nànuchi'i Shį

DÄN K'E TRANSLATIONS

(Southern Tutchone Translations)

Family

Ấdzų̈a — My Sweetheart
Ấghàałan — My Family
Ấghats'èa — Woman's Daugher
Ấghra — Woman's Son
Ấmbada – My Sister (Older)
Ấmbē — My Auntie (Dad's Side)
Ấndaya — My Brother (Older)
Ấshèa Ke — Great-Grandchildren
Ấtà — My Dad
Ấtàya — My Uncle (Dad's side)
Ấtsía — My Grandpa
Ấtsųą — My Grandma
Ấtsų Khįą — My Great-Grandma

Animals

Kwấntsì Mèn — Spider Web

Colour

Dädäla — Orange
Däk'äl — White
Däts'al — Grey
Dät'äl — Red
Dätthäw — Yellow
Jänäch'ür — Black
Jänǹthù — Brown
Jänńtl'ą̈rą — Blue
Khàdlų̄ Dädäla — Pink

Feelings

Jenída — I Am Sick/Sad
Nìzhat — Nervous
Uyètaákwätth'ät — Not Paying Attention

Food

Ätthän Gän — Dried Meat
Łu Gän — Dried Fish

Greetings

Nànuchi'i Shį — See You Later
Shäw Níthän — Thank You

Medicine

K'ày — Willow

People

Ätsk'ia — Mary Shadow
Chùschwa — Marge Jackson
Däts'ä'la — Jenny Moose
Gáts'äda — Delmer MacDonald
Lasänmą — Mariah MacDonald
Ts'ùk'aymą —
Agnes MacDonald-Sutton

Places

Ấkų̀ — Home
Äzįzha — Moon
Dákwäkäda — Haines Junction
Keyi — City
K'uą Män — Kloo Lake
Kwänlin — Whitehorse
Łu Ghą— Klukshu
Nàday Gän — Mount Decoeli
Tsí Män — Pine Lake

DENE TRANSLATIONS

Setsų Cho — My Great-Grandma
Setsų — My Grandma
Semo — My Mom
Semoó — My Auntie (Mom's Side)
Dehcho — Big River or Mackenzie River
Godéeah — Mariah MacDonald
Mahsi Cho — Thank You
Zhahti Kų́ę́ — Fort Providence
K'ágee — Kakisa Lake

ACKNOWLEDGEMENTS

i wouldn't be who i am if it wasn't for my Ä́ghàałan who raised me. for Semo for always being there for me no matter what (so much so that she's holds the title as being the first editor of these poems). for Ä́tà who raised me to the best of his ability. to both of them for doing their best to keep their children free from the traumas that they experienced, and for raising Ä́mbada and i on the land and enriched in our indigenous culture. from sewing, to dancing, to trapping, or fishing, Semo and Ä́tà gave me the keys to healing in my culture, and the path to avoid the troubles they endured. for Ä́tsųą and Ä́tsía for always having my back, and for Ä́mbē and Ä́tàya who continue to have my back today. thank you to Lisa Jacobs (aunty candy) for helping me with finding the Southern Tutchone words for my poems. thank you to the community and the land that raised me. for the elders who continue to inspire me, to the elders who left impressions in my life. to those who passed on, thank you to Jenny Moose, Agnes MacDonald-Sutton, Delmer MacDonald, Marge Jackson, & Mary Shadow for their influence, and knowledge, may they rest peacefully. for the mountains that watched over me throughout my youth. for the rez dogs that would either chase me or play with me on village rds, and in my front yard. to my first rez dog Joker who inspired me to begin writing when i was six. to my upbringing that continue to inspire me in my twenties.

i want to thank my family in nwt. though i haven't spent much time on those flat lands. i remember my visits fondly. thank you to my loving family of the Dehcho, for always being welcoming to me whenever i visit, whether i was eight or twenty-five, you all were always happy to have us, and i hope that one day i can visit more often, and even enrich myself in the culture of my maternal line. i want to thank Semoó Sheryl Yakeleya & Doris Camsell for helping me with finding Dene words for my poems. you really helped me in my writing about the Dehcho, and the beautiful land surrounding it.

i want to thank the city of Vancouver for helping me find the beauty of the Yukon. i moved there in the hopes of finding new life, in the hopes of starting something different. thank you Vancouver for making so depressed and miserable that i began to appreciate the life i lived on the land. for inspiring the late night poem-writing sessions that i used to combat the homesickness that i endured during the four long years i lived under the rain clouds and city lights.

i want to thank Brick Books for reading my poems and seeing my potential. for giving me the chance to share my poems and culture. i want thank Wanda John-Kehewin for helping with the first rounds of editing. i want to thank Alayna Munce and Manahil Bandukwala for taking extra care with my poems and helping me with the last rounds of editing.

lastly, i want to thank you for reading. i hope you enjoyed reading about my culture, the land, my childhood, and my struggle into adulthood. i appreciate you, the reader, for taking the time to choose my book, spending the money, using your library card, or borrowing this book from your friend. thank you for giving your free time to read my stories. i greatly appreciate it!

Shäw Níthän/Mahsi Cho,

Lasänmą/Godééah

Mariah MacDonald

Lasänmą (she/her) was raised in Haines Junction, Yukon and is a member of the Champagne and Aishihik First Nation. Her English name is Mariah MacDonald, and she is a part of the Wolf Clan. Lasänmą lived in Haines Junction and Whitehorse before moving to Vancouver at the age of twenty-one, where she studied at the University of British Columbia (located on the unceded Territories of the Musqueam, Squamish and Tsleil-Waututh First Nations). *Spruce to Cedar* is Lasänmą's first published work as an author.

Printed by Imprimerie Gauvin
Gatineau, Québec